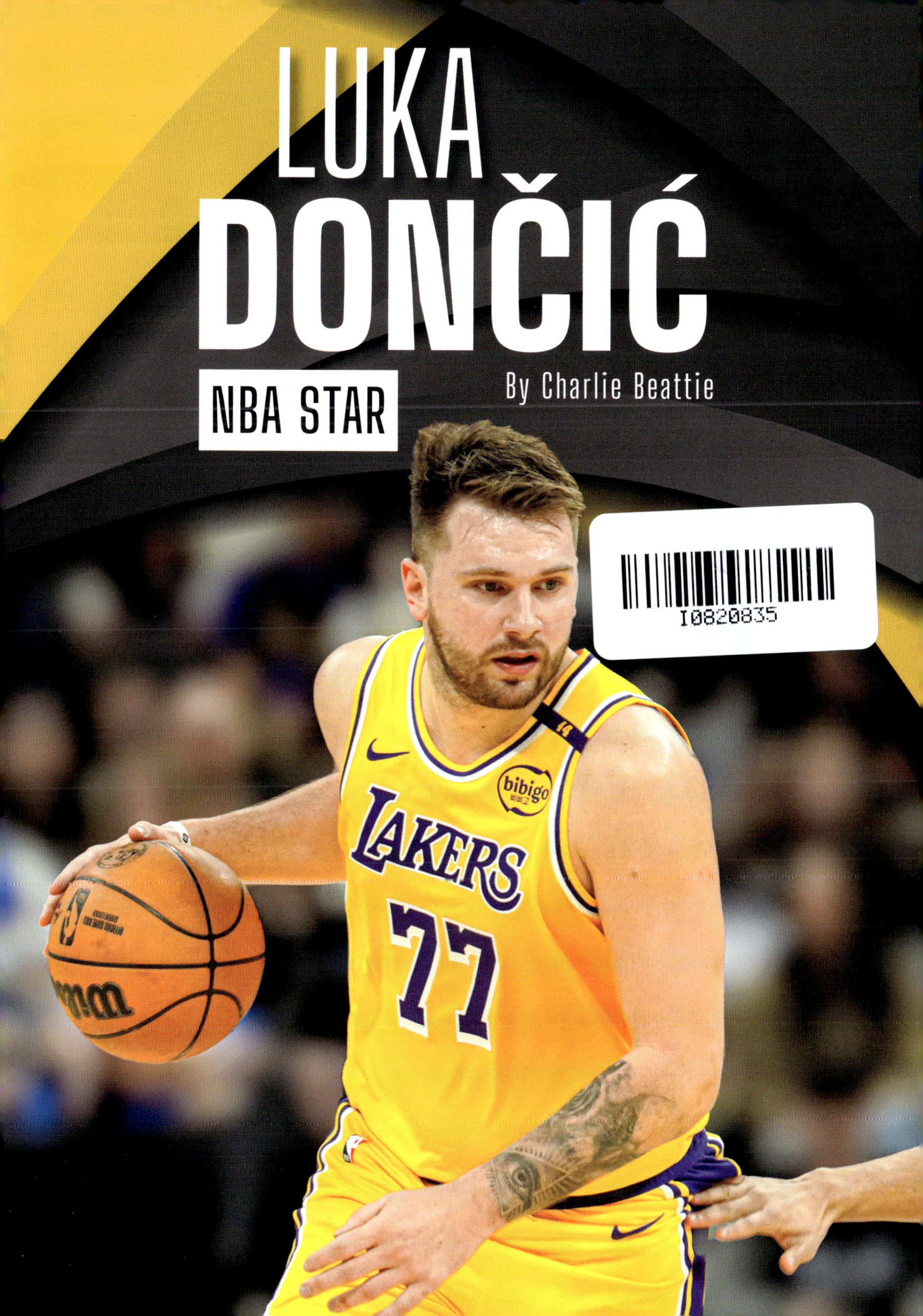
LUKA
DONČIĆ
NBA STAR
By Charlie Beattie
I0820835
bibigo
LAKERS
77

Book design by Jake Nordby
Cover design by Jake Nordby

Photographs ©: Marty Jean-Louis/Sipa USA/AP Images, cover, 1; LM Otero/AP Images, 4, 23; Sam Hodde/Getty Images Sport/Getty Images, 6–7, 8; Sonia Canada/Getty Images Sport/Getty Images, 10; Richard Rodriguez/Getty Images Sport/Getty Images, 13; Mitchell Leff/Getty Images Sport/Getty Images, 14; Ashley Landis/AP Images, 16; David Berding/Getty Images Sport/Getty Images, 19; Michael Reaves/Getty Images Sport/Getty Images, 21; Red Line Editorial, 22

Press Box Books, an imprint of Press Room Editions.

Library of Congress Control Number: 2025942810

ISBN
979-8-89469-067-4 (library bound)
979-8-89469-076-6 (paperback)
979-8-89469-093-3 (epub)
979-8-89469-085-8 (hosted ebook)

Distributed by North Star Editions, Inc.
2297 Waters Drive
Mendota Heights, MN 55120
www.northstareditions.com

Printed in the United States of America
012026

ABOUT THE AUTHOR

Charlie Beattie is a writer, editor, and former sportscaster. Originally from Saint Paul, Minnesota, he now lives in Charleston, South Carolina, with his wife and son.

TABLE OF CONTENTS

NBA
77
GET
THE
13

1

BACK TO DALLAS

Basketball fans received shocking news on February 2, 2025. The Dallas Mavericks had traded one of the top stars in the National Basketball Association (NBA). They sent Luka Dončić to the Los Angeles Lakers.

Dončić had been the Mavericks' best player since his rookie season in 2018–19. Fans in Dallas loved him. And just a year earlier, the Slovenian guard had led the

Luka Dončić recorded eight rebounds and six assists in his first game back in Dallas as a Laker.

Dončić holds back tears as he's introduced before his first game in Dallas as a Laker.

Mavericks to the NBA Finals. As a result, the trade upset many fans in Dallas.

On April 9, the Lakers visited Dallas for the first time since the big trade. The Mavericks played a video tribute to Dončić before the

game. Also, each fan received a shirt that read *Hvala za vse*. In Slovenian, that means “Thank you for everything.”

Fans cheered every time Dončić touched the ball. Just over a minute into the game, Dončić sank his first basket. He drove to the

Dončić shoots over his former teammate Dereck Lively II.

middle of the lane and stopped. Then he hit a one-handed floater. Dallas supporters let out a roar.

Dončić drained shots with ease throughout the game. He had scored 14 points by the end of the first quarter. He mixed drives to the basket with deep three-point shots. By halftime, Dončić had racked up 31 points. And the Dallas crowd was still cheering every basket.

The Lakers cruised to a 112–97 win. With 1:34 left, Dončić came out of the game. Fans gave him a standing ovation. Dončić clapped to them as he left the floor.

FOR AND AGAINST

Dončić scored 45 points against the Mavericks. That matched his highest point total of the 2024–25 season. Dončić had also scored 45 while playing for Dallas earlier in the season. It was just the second time in NBA history that a player had scored 45 points for and against the same team in a single season.

38.4
7
Teka
11
EA7
EMPORIO ARMANI
air.es

2

LUKA MAGIC

Luka Dončić was born on February 28, 1999. He grew up in Ljubljana, Slovenia. His father, Saša, played professional basketball. Luka developed basketball skills quickly. He was too skilled for his age group. So, he had to play against older kids in Slovenia.

Real Madrid noticed his talent. When Luka was 13, the Spanish club signed him to its youth team. Three years later, Luka

Luka Dončić played 216 games for Real Madrid.

joined the senior team. He was the youngest senior player in club history. Real Madrid played in a league with teams from all over Europe. In 2017–18, Dončić led his team to the league title. He earned Most Valuable Player (MVP) honors. At 19, he became the youngest player to ever win the award.

NBA teams watched Dončić closely. Scouts ranked him as one of the top players in the 2018 draft. The Atlanta Hawks picked him third overall that year. However, the Hawks traded him to the Dallas Mavericks on draft night.

Dončić succeeded in the NBA right away. He could score in many ways. Dončić used his

NATIONAL PRIDE

EuroBasket is a tournament between the best national teams in Europe. Entering 2017, Slovenia had never won it. But the small country upset Serbia 93–85 in the final that year. Dončić scored eight points in the game. He also grabbed seven rebounds.

NBA scouts loved Dončić's passing ability.

As a rookie, Dončić led the Mavericks in scoring.

6-foot-6 (198-cm), 230-pound (104-kg) frame to outmuscle smaller defenders. Opponents had to guard him closely. If they gave Dončić space, he'd drain a three-pointer. On top of scoring, Dončić also dished out clever passes. He hustled for rebounds, too.

In December 2018, the Mavericks faced the Houston Rockets. Dallas trailed 102–94 with three minutes left. Dončić hit a three-pointer from the corner. The rookie buried another three-pointer on his next shot. Then he drove for a short jump shot. The next time down the floor, Dončić nailed another three-pointer. He had scored 11 straight points. The Mavericks won 107–104.

Dončić had many other great performances during his first year in the NBA. After the season ended, he won the Rookie of the Year Award.

3

A BIG DEAL

Luka Dončić played in his first NBA playoff game in August 2020. Facing the Los Angeles Clippers, Dončić made 13 of his 21 shots. He ended the game with 42 points. No NBA player had ever scored more in his first playoff game. But it wasn't enough. The Mavericks lost 118–110.

Dončić could seemingly do it all. Starting in 2019–20, he made the All-NBA First Team five years in a row. He often

Dončić scored more than 30 points in three different games during his first playoff series.

earned votes for the MVP Award. And he broke many Dallas records. His combination of skills helped him tally plenty of triple-doubles, too. In a 2022 game, Dončić had 60 points, 21 rebounds, and 10 assists.

INCREDIBLE NIGHT

Dončić lit up the Atlanta Hawks on January 26, 2024. The Mavericks guard set a team record with 73 points. It was the fourth-highest scoring total in NBA history. Dončić also finished the game with 7 assists and 10 rebounds.

Dončić usually stepped up his game in the playoffs. In 2022, no player averaged more points per game in the postseason than Dončić. His scoring led the Mavericks to the Western Conference finals. They hadn't advanced that far in 11 years. However, the Golden State Warriors ended their run.

Two years later, Dončić lifted the Mavericks back to the Western Conference finals. They

Dončić takes the winning shot in Game 2 of the 2024 Western Conference finals.

faced the Minnesota Timberwolves. In Game 2, Dallas trailed 108–106 with only three seconds left. The Mavericks put the ball in Dončić's hands. He hit a game-winning three-pointer to silence the Minnesota crowd. The Mavericks went on to win the series in five games.

Dallas took on the Boston Celtics in the NBA Finals. Dončić put up a triple-double in Game 2. And he scored at least 27 points in every game of the series. However, the Celtics won the Finals in five games.

Dallas fans believed Dončić could lead the team to a championship. But he had trouble staying healthy. His injuries frustrated Dallas's general manager. So, the Mavericks traded their star to the Los Angeles Lakers in February 2025.

Dončić was crushed. He loved Dallas and its fans. Even so, he continued to shine for the Lakers. He led the team to the 2025 playoffs. It didn't matter what team he played for. Dončić continued to be one of the NBA's top stars.

Dončić averaged 28.2 points per game with the Lakers in 2025.

TIMELINE MAP

1. **Ljubljana, Slovenia: 1999**
   Luka Dončić is born on February 28.
2. **Madrid, Spain: 2015**
   Dončić makes his professional debut for Real Madrid.
3. **Brooklyn, New York: 2018**
   The Atlanta Hawks select Dončić with the third pick in the draft. The Dallas Mavericks then trade for him on draft night.
4. **Dallas, Texas: 2019**
   Dončić wins the NBA's Rookie of the Year Award for the 2018–19 season.
5. **Lake Buena Vista, Florida: 2020**
   Dončić sets an NBA record with 42 points in his playoff debut.
6. **Atlanta, Georgia: 2024**
   Dončić sets a Dallas record by scoring 73 points against the Atlanta Hawks.
7. **Minneapolis, Minnesota: 2024**
   Dončić hits a game-winning shot with three seconds left in Game 2 of the Western Conference finals. Dallas goes on to win the series against the Minnesota Timberwolves.
8. **Los Angeles, California: 2025**
   The Mavericks trade Dončić to the Los Angeles Lakers.

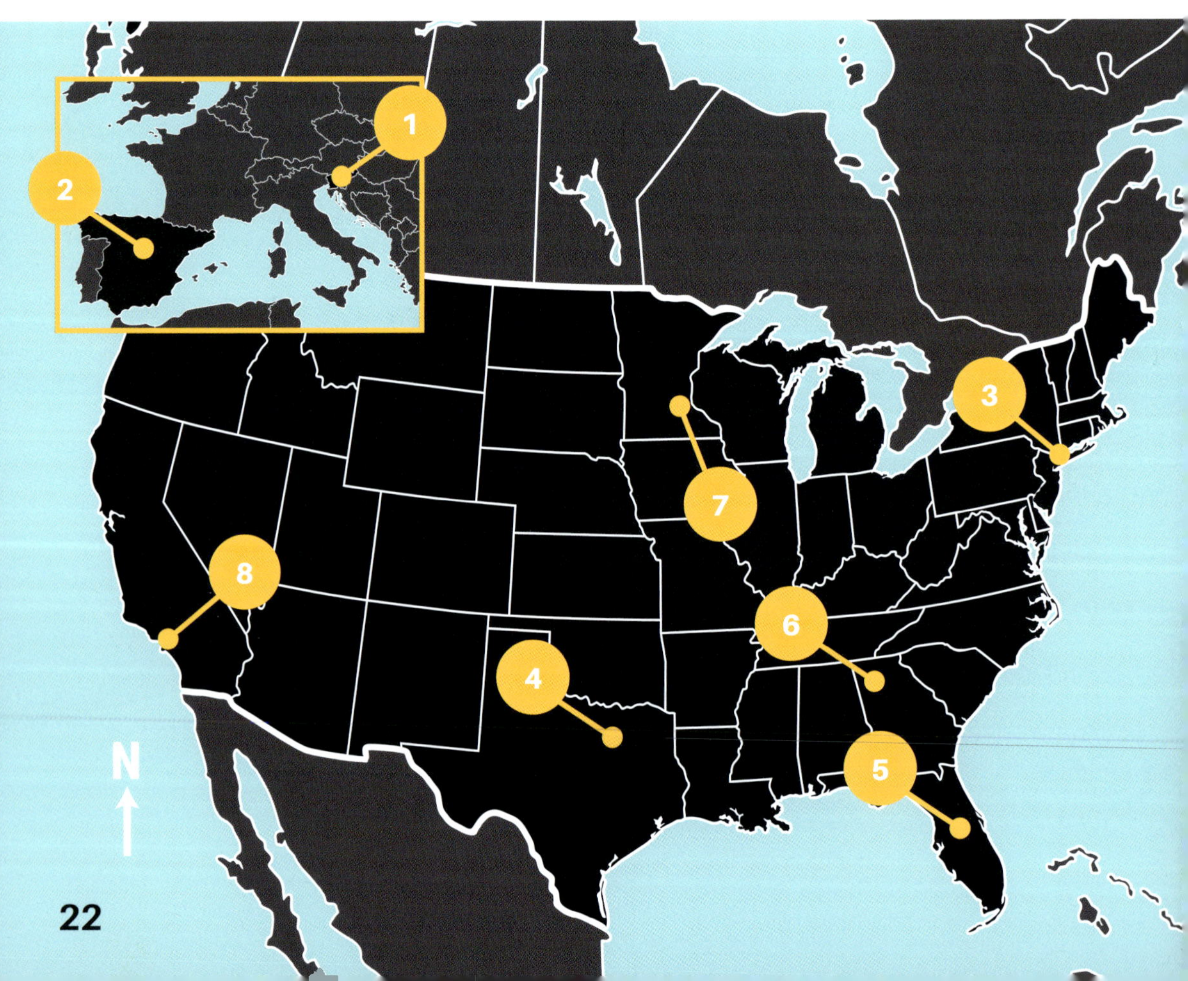

AT A GLANCE

LUKA DONČIĆ

Birth date: February 28, 1999

Birthplace: Ljubljana, Slovenia

Position: Guard

Height: 6-foot-6 (198-cm)

Weight: 230 pounds (104 kg)

Current team: Los Angeles Lakers (2025-)

Past teams: Dallas Mavericks (2018–25), Real Madrid (2015–18)

Major awards: NBA Rookie of the Year (2019), All-NBA First Team (2020, 2021, 2022, 2023, 2024), NBA All-Star (2020, 2021, 2022, 2023, 2024), NBA scoring title (2024)

Accurate through the 2024–25 season.

MORE INFORMATION

To learn more about Luka Dončić, go to **pressboxbooks.com/AllAccess**.

These links are routinely monitored and updated to provide the most current information available.

GLOSSARY

assists
Passes that lead directly to a teammate scoring a basket.

draft
An event that allows teams to choose new players coming into the league.

general manager
The person in a team's front office who drafts and signs new players.

ovation
A show of appreciation, such as cheering or clapping.

scouts
People who look for talented young players.

senior team
The highest level of a club.

tribute
An act that shows gratitude or respect for a person or group.

triple-doubles
When a player reaches 10 or more of three different statistics in one game.

INDEX